A Zodiac-Wisdom Book for K

OVERCOME BULLYING, FIN
HARMONY, AND TAKE BACK YOUR POWER.

Key Life Lessons for ALL Home, School, and Social/Peer Group Scenarios

GRACE GABRIELLA PUSKAS

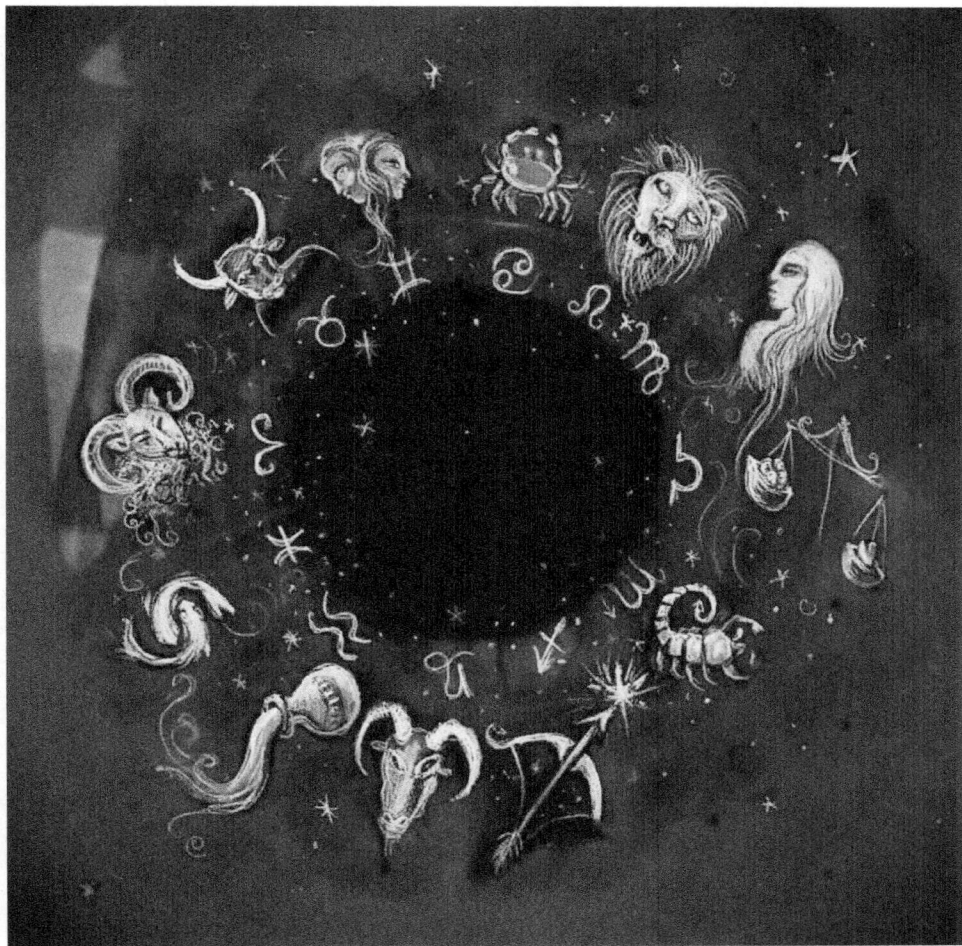

INTRODUCTION

Sometimes in this world, life isn't fair,
sometimes we're given tests and challenges to make us stare
into space, wondering, 'why is this happening to me?'
Well, there's a lesson in the hard times, you see.

Just a like a diamond, one of the most beautiful crystals,
We must face pressure to transform and evolve... to reach new levels.
Diamonds are one of the rarest gemstones to be found,
yet they form over thousands of years, they don't just pop up from the ground

This is what Astrology teaches us, the stars up above-
Heaven is a place on earth and in our hearts.
Your Star Sign will tell you many, many secrets,
Guiding you to your highest potential and truest wisdom.

Self-knowledge, learning, and, of course, fun, are available in this book;
I am an Owl in human disguise sent to change the way you look,
feel, sense, observe, and interact with the world...
I am merely a messenger to the Spirit world.

What is Spirit, you may be wondering, well, Spirit is the invisible energy,
it's in *everything*, every human, animal, and tree.
Spirit is the missing link that you will one day come to see as a gift,
but first you must understand that Astrology is a link to the Infinite.

Your Star Sign speaks of your core strengths, it shapes your personality,
your weaknesses, gifts, talents, likes and dislikes, and personal identity!
It's a direct gateway to you becoming the best version of yourself, *self-mastery*,
so, remember this when you feel down or lost... there's hidden wisdom your
physical eyes can't see.

✧

For you adults, you can visit my Youtube Channel the ***Dream & Spirit Weaver*** for FREE educational videos, wisdom sharings, and spiritual/holistic/esoteric teachings.
(https://www.youtube.com/@TheDreamSpiritWeaver)

✧

ABOUT THE AUTHOR

Grace Gabriella Puskas is a spiritual author of two groundbreaking collections of poetry and a creative visionary. She won the 2014 Local Legend National Writing Competition, which began her journey as a poet, writer, and author. She is a world-class ghost-writer, helping individuals, healers, charities, businesses, and celebrities bring their vision to fruition. Grace is a Top Rated freelancer on Upwork, the world's biggest freelancing platform, as well as passionate and qualified Reiki Master Teacher, Dream therapist, Crystal & Shamanic Healer, Chi Kung practitioner, Reflexologist, Aromatherapist, and Herbalist. Grace has spent time volunteering on various projects; spiritual, conscious, eco/sustainable, community, and animal welfare and conservation, and has lived on organic farms, and in shamanic land communities and ashrams. Her spirituality is authentic! She is a top Astrologer who enjoys tuning into the invisible realms of Spirit and the ether to birth "blueprints of the self."

Grace is a Pisces with a Grand Water Trine *and* Grand Earth Trine in her birth chart, two rare astrological alignments. This creates an actual *Diamond*, and is very rare… Grace believes we can transcend comfort zones by leaving behind a fear timeline, and moving towards a timeline of LOVE; astrology, poetry, and embracing new philosophies are part of this. She is a Pisces Sun, Cancer Moon, and Taurus Rising.

You can contact Grace at: gracegabriella33@gmail.com

https://gracegabriella33.wixsite.com/grace
https://www.youtube.com/@TheDreamSpiritWeaver

"We are the Rainbow Generation,
the light split into color due to the physicality of observation;
The One harmonious sound being distorted through differing notes...
Musical vibrations in a magical dance,
awakening from a repetitive trance,
which the imbalance has created,
throughout all times and ages!"

- GRACE GABRIELLA PUSKAS

ABOUT THE ARTIST

Husna Lohiya is a passionate artist and illustrator who believes in the continuous, perpetual, and multifaceted nature of our physical world. She embraces diverse themes, spirituality, and the importance of pattern, culture, and community. Her complexity, yet divine simplicity with her art gives her creations a unique and coherent language; her paintings and illustrations capture many existential conditions. For example, merging nature, personality, and the self! Husna has won prestigious awards including the Mumbai Hero award, as well as being a competition winner on Channel 4's "Drawers Off." She believes this is a testament to who she is as an artist.

In Husna's words: "I am a visionary artist who weaves the tapestry of existence through brush strokes! I love to create worlds where spirituality, culture, and nature converge in harmonious beauty…"

You can contact Husna at: **hus-lo@hotmail.com**
or by visiting her Facebook page, **'Happyhusna Henna.'**

Contents

ARIES: The Ram

Key qualities: Ambitious, determined, passionate, zestful, energetic, resourceful, intelligent, intuitive, innovative, original, energetic, willful, confident, courageous, fiery, independent, self-autonomous, and optimistic.

Weaknesses/Shadow traits to watch out for: Overly dominant and forceful, egotistical, bullyish, impatient, impulsive, brutal, a tyrant!, insensitive, very argumentative, a lack of empathy + humility, stubborn; embarks on a war-path

COMPATIBLE Star Signs: Aries, Gemini, Leo, Libra, Sagittarius, and Aquarius

INCOMPATIBLE, where there will be least harmony: Cancer, Virgo, and Pisces

Did you know that Rams take charge, often bulldozing over others?
They are so powerfully assertive and direct that they often cause chaos.
They are headstrong, willful, courageous, and strong-willed,
yet this makes them bullies who over-dominate and create ill...

Ill-intentions, ill-wishes, harm, and hurtful actions
make Aries, the Ram, a powerful leader but simultaneous tyrant!
They are dictators, overly forceful, aggressive, and domineering,
so more sensitive and emotional creatures tend to live in fear around their sneering.

Of course, not all Rams are mean, it's just a personality flaw you need to watch out for;
they get on with Sagittarius the Archer, Gemini the Twins, and Leo the Lion more!
Also Aquarius the Water-Bearer and their opposite sign, Libra, the Scales-
Other signs may have a trickier time dealing with the Ram who can't be tamed...

Aries is wild, independent, liberated, and fiercely stubborn,
You don't want to mess with this untamed beast when they're on a path of destruction.
Aries is ruled by the God and planet of war, Mars himself,
This means they thrive in competition, want to win, and desire nothing more than to be seen as the best.

Aries the Ram is a headstrong and noble creature when at their best, but they sometimes play out their shadow,
becoming too dominant, unkind, insensitive, and making people feel mellow.
They are the bullies of the zodiac who put themselves first every time,
remember this when you feel it's only fair to be given a chance to shine.

See, Aries craves the spotlight, they need to be number 1,
they're high-flying, ambitious, determined, and sing their own song.
They possess powerful life force, energy levels, and vitality,

but earth and water signs tend to get lost to this Ram's uncontrollable lack of humility.

Aries is not too humble- sensitivity and modesty aren't they're greatest gifts,
In fact, they can be monstrous jerks and gits!
They are the natural born leaders who seek to win at all costs,
Be careful, stand your ground, and try to show them the true meaning of friendship & love.

Because the Ram is an instinctive animal with raw and primal emotions,
This means their temper is unmatched- they can be explosive.
Aries will pull a temper tantrum, scream to win, or stomp all over you,
they don't care if they're being argumentative, mean, or rude.

It's all about them, they need to be admired and seen as 'number 1,'
there's no such thing as harmony, teamwork, or a gentle and empathic touch.
As the warrior who is ruled by the god of war,
Aries is sinister and mean-spirited, they will smile at your fall!

It's true, they are competitive beyond belief, so take note;
this is the most arrogant sign who will smile and gloat
at your suffering, they take joy from your pain,
As they are very ambitious, they wish to rise to fortune and fame.

But fame at the expense of friendship is not healthy, so perhaps you can teach them this:
Life is not about hostility, aggression, or conflict.
It's not about outshining others or throwing them under the bus,
Aries' lesson is to rise in grace and humility, to embody universal love.

TAURUS: The Bull

Key qualities: Romantic, sweet, loyal, dependable, practical, down-to-earth, responsible, dutiful, reliable, nurturing, kind, trustworthy, faithful, a lover at heart, an amazing friend, intelligent, empathic, mature, grounded, imaginative, logical, sensual, tenacious, wise, discerning, and honest.

Weaknesses/Shadow traits to watch out for: Extreme stubbornness, inflexibility, laziness, inertia, a lack of get-up and go, possessiveness, and uncompromising.

COMPATIBLE Star Signs: Taurus, Cancer, Virgo, Scorpio, Capricorn, and Pisces

INCOMPATIBLE, where there will be least harmony: Leo, Sagittarius, and Aquarius

I am Taurus, the Bull! This means I see red,
I am quick to anger with a real temper when forced out of bed.
I love to sleep, you see, I am one of the most lazy around-
I am unmotivated, idle, and prone to being home-bound.

I love my sleep, I love to rest, and I enjoy eating comfort foods,
It helps to keep me passive and serene, but puts me in a real mood.
Like the Bull, anything that disrupts my bubble of comfort or safe haven
is charged at with vitality, passion, and a rage that's not cool or welcome.

I am usually calm, cool, and kind- I am very friendly and affectionate,
but desire for pleasure keeps me trapped in a bad spiral.
Unlike others, I choose comfort and security over fun and play,
I could happily laze around eating my favorite foods every day…

But this doesn't help me in the long-run, it only serves as instant gratification,
which prevents me from evolving or developing my mind and education.
My emotions suffer too, and this creates disharmony in all my relationships,
from school to home, parents to peers, and even among my love interests!

As the most lazy and comfort-seeking sign, I take pleasure in material things,
when at my best I am wise, practical, dependable, responsible, and able to
sing;
I have many creative and artistic talents, so I should be imaginative daily,
remember this when you see me wallowing in doubt or self-pity.

If you are a Taurus, take note of your shadow, your less desirable traits,
as these are what lead to your greatest defeat.
You have a hard time letting go of ideas, beliefs, and old cycles,
so your key lesson is to move on gracefully, accept life involves obstacles.

You can't always control what cannot be changed- sometimes we win,
sometimes we lose;
and you can't tell others how to walk in their own shoes.
You can motivate, be inspirational, and guide, lead, or teach,

but as the Bull you are stubborn beyond belief, you have a real possessive
streak!

So, I am Taurus the Bull, a sensual earth sign who loves to eat,
to sing, draw, paint, be creative, sleep, and watch t.v.
I must remember to tap into my innate intelligence, emotional sensitivity, and
empathy,
Only then will I be an amazing friend among my friendship groups + family.

Because I am really humble, I am modest and down-to-earth,
I fill others with inspiration, kindness, and positive words.
When at the top of my game I am the most amazing friend,
Yet at my worst? I drive others around the bend.

I am so inflexible and stubborn that I can make people move backwards and
stop still…
You see, I have incredible force, perseverance, and will.
This means I know how to make decisions and set plans in motions,
The only problem is, when in my shadow, I lack devotion.

I am usually calm, peace-loving, harmonious, and serene,
but when pushed or triggered my anger is seen...
I become rageful and explosive, reacting from instincts,
I am impatient and impulsive without the ability to think.

I feel things, deeply, I want to be seen as benevolent,
as kind, loving, loyal, generous, and compassionate.
And I am these things, I am one of the best friends to have,
but when this Bull sees red, well, you should make other plans.

Be careful, stand your ground, and walk away with grace,
Ignore my reactiveness and keep a smile on your face.
All I need is a few moments to calm down and think rationally,
then you'll see that I truly am one of the most down-to-earth, with sincerity.

GEMINI: The Twins

Key qualities: Logical, analytical, rational, intuitive, bright, witty, highly intelligent, persuasive, an excellent communicator, imaginative, observant, perceptive, a problem-solver and solution-finder, humorous, fun-loving, playful, energetic, optimistic, enthusiastic, curious, inquisitive, social, expressive, youthful, and charming.

Weaknesses/Shadow traits to watch out for: Superficial, impulsive, impractical, sarcastic, fidgety, frivolous, unfaithful, scattered, impatient, insensitive, lacks empathy and emotional depth & vulnerability, and deceptive.

COMPATIBLE Star Signs: Aries, Gemini, Leo, Libra, Sagittarius, and Aquarius.

INCOMPATIBLE, where there will be least harmony: Scorpio, Capricorn, and Pisces

I am Gemini, the Twins, the symbol for the trickster,
I love to gossip and talk and am a real practical joker!
This is bad, I take being sociable too far,
I don't know how to tone it down or stop spreading rumors, it's too hard.

See, I am ruled by Mercury, the planet of communication,
This gives me excellent wit, mentality clarity, and powers of observation.
I am perceptive, logical, analytical, insightful, and wise,
I choose not to feel, but to think and use my mind...

I am very analytical, rational, and overly concerned with humor,
I have a real hard time accepting there are other gifts to choose from,
like emotions, instincts, empathy, sensitivity, or gentleness,
I find joy in another person's suffering then throw it in their face.

It's a horrible trait to possess, I lack kindness and compassion
because my mind takes over, I see endless chances for distraction.
Gossip is my worst quality, as well as spreading mistruths-
I can be extremely reckless, unhelpful, and rude!

Lacking sensitivity combined with an overactive mind
makes me seek fun, play, and adventure... every time.
I lack grounding, sensibility, respect for adults, and the ability to be quiet,
which makes me into a trickster, an evil mastermind, and a tyrant.

Also, like a robot, I lack emotional vulnerability, soul, and depth,
I will always choose humor, lightness, logic, and wit.
This let's me be the life and soul of a party- I'm a social chameleon,
but I'm not the most trustworthy or loyal human when it comes to other's feelings...

I like to make others submit to my plots, I scheme up plans to destroy,
I create chaos and mayhem and treat others as my toys.
I am not a bad person, but I see life as a game,
so I must learn to balance emotions and sensitivity with my highly evolved brain.

Because I am the one sign linked to false speech,
Spreading rumors, finding joy from others' suffering, and lying through greed.
I have a big ego, which makes me want to be seen as superior-
I think I can observe, perceive, and analyze better than every other human.

I am an excellent storyteller, and when at my best, this makes me amazing,
I have extraordinary gifts of communication and persuasion!
But, when in my shadow- my lowest, I am merely full of slander,
I gossip, lie, and spread mistruths to make me appear better.

If you don't know, Mercury is the planet of communication, and this is my ruler.
So, I can be impulsive, impatient, and engage in reckless behavior.
I play the class clown, yet at extreme levels;
I'm not very sensible, practical, or dependable.

My lesson in life is to uncover truth,
Only then will I be more trusting to you.
I bully others through my sharp with and humor,
even making teachers and adults submit to me, it's unheard of...

I am one of the rare few who can gain respect through my mind,
I can be deceptive and manipulative, so I know what to say in perfect time.
I also know the right things to say, and this makes me dominant,
while appearing intelligent, I am really being unkind.

Like the evil mastermind, I embody the energy of a poltergeist,
I may be deeply bright, but I'm not very gracious or nice.
I like to play jokes on others and laugh at their despair,
I may be here to teach you that life isn't always fair.

As a dominant yang sign, I am overpowering, very confident, and charming,
Yet I lack emotional vulnerability and sensitivity, and can be deceptive and domineering.
This means I am superficial, I say what I think others want me to hear,
Therefore I need to rise from the depths of manipulation and let go of cunning and fear.

CANCER: The Crab

Key qualities: Sensitive, dreamy, compassionate, loving, loyal, kind, empathic, nurturing, caring, artistic, imaginative, creative, psychic, spiritually gifted, domestic, responsible, intuitive, instinctive, emotionally mature and deep, wise, unconditionally loving, protective, providing, sentimental, home-loving, and selfless.

Weaknesses/Shadow traits to watch out for: Clingy, codependent, moody, withdrawn, super-sensitive and hyper-emotional, mood swings, prone to depression, pessimistic, manipulative, and self-sacrificing.

COMPATIBLE Star Signs: Taurus, Cancer, Virgo, Scorpio, Capricorn, and Pisces

INCOMPATIBLE, where there will be least harmony: Aries, Leo, and Sagittarius

I am Cancer, the caring yet moody Crab,
I am the most moody and mellow star sign, so take note when I'm feeling bad!
I can ruin a party, social outing, or mood,
I'm one of the least bullyish signs, but I can be withdrawn and crude.

As the Crab, I find more comfort in emotions and feelings,
the sea is my home- I only come up to land to peak in
to the world of humans, I find more solace amongst the sea creatures,
remember this when you try to turn to me as your teacher...

I am wise, imaginative, artistically gifted, and incredibly compassionate,
I'm also an amazing friend- nurturing and highly instinctive.
However, I can be deeply shy, reserved, and introspective,
which means I like my own company- I often break down to be reflective.

I'm not very good at talking nor do I use my voice to connect,
I am sad, unhappy, lonely, and somewhat depressed!
I like my own company due to feeling lost in the big wide world,
when at my best I am the most wonderful friend, but at other times I'm the worst.

See, I thrive in the realm of emotions, feelings, and subtle sensations,
at parties I get lost, I'm even bullied and isolated...
I am the sign most likely to play victim, yet, the truth is, I can be manipulative,
This means I may not be overpowering, but I'm not completely innocent.

As one of the most imaginative and sensitive signs I prefer to make music,
to draw, paint, write poetry, sit in nature, or express my feelings.
I prefer company in small groups, and I don't like large crowds,
This makes me a victim in cliques and to those who are confident and loud.

If I do ever turn bullyish, it's only because I'm tired of everyone bitching,
of sitting in a social circle gossiping and hating.
As the Great Nurturer and Caregiver who is incredibly introspective,
my only real folly is being slightly negative!

It's true, I can be pessimistic and self-pitying,
Giving into feelings of hopelessness, despair, and false vision.
I want everything to be dreamy and full of love, rainbows, and unicorns,
Yet unicorns aren't real, they only exist in my mind's imaginative
playground...

Don't ever accuse me of bullying, though, as this is when you'll see my
fiercely protective side,
I can be passive aggressive, which means I'll explode with repressed pride.
I take immense pride in my ability to protect, serve, and be instinctive-
I am a symbol for family and home, so never belittle my feelings.

As, like the Kraken who arises from the sea,
You may come to find fire can be put out by sensitivity.
My modesty, gentleness, emotional depth, and compassion
are saintlike, but even the Archangels cause destruction!

I live for my friends and family, but I will occasionally snap,
Like the mighty ocean I sometimes want to make my power known.
I am not forceful or dominant, my waves are gentle,
and it's only sporadically that I pop up from my shell; I'm less aggressive,
more sentimental.

My talents are usually overlooked to bigger personalities, so remember this;
I may be shy, withdrawn, and introverted, but my pincers truly pinch!
What does this mean? Well, it means I may be the most gentle and passive,
Yet I will defend myself... this Crab is not dinner in a restaurant.

LEO: The Lion

Key qualities: Noble, regal, charming, intelligent, intuitive, original, sociable, friendly, gregarious, benevolent, kind, generous, romantic, charismatic, elegant, determined, courageous, responsible, ambitious, loyal, proud, excitable, enthusiastic, creative, innovative, expressive, and passionate.

Weaknesses/Shadow traits to watch out for: Overly proud, a real drama queen/king!- domineering, overpowering, smug, self-entitled, selfish, bossy, massive ego, attention-seeking, bullyish, and seeks control over others.

COMPATIBLE Star Signs: Aries, Gemini, Leo, Libra, Sagittarius, and Aquarius

INCOMPATIBLE, where there will be least harmony: Taurus, Cancer, and Scorpio

I am Leo, the official bully of the zodiac. Oh no!
This means I am dominant, overpowering, and put on a show.
I love the spotlight, there's nothing more I crave,
I am self-authoritative, noble, regal, queen/king of the jungle, and head of the game.

I am a dominant and fiery creature, which means I take charge,
I command presence and attention, I always act like the star…
This has its positives and setbacks, as I can be completely self-centered,
I don't know how to let others shine and act like a nasty preacher.

I am self-righteous, self-entitled, egotistical, mean-spirited, and totally selfish,
If you have gifts or talents, good luck letting other people know it!
See, I am the center of the zodiac, also ruled by the Sun,
This means I love to be the best, to shine, and be seen as "the One…"

The best or the most beautiful, talented, or amazing,
I am incapable of humility, which is being humble, modest, and negotiating.
I lack diplomacy and gentless, grace is not my strength,
As a natural born leader I make demands, I live to outshine the rest.

I am kind, generous, romantic, noble, and charming, however,
I have many friends and admirers- I am a highly sociable creature...
When at the top of my game I am loved and respected by many,
It's unfortunate that my massive ego gets in the way of harmony and humility.

I bulldoze over others, I like to make them feel small and weak,
I find it hard to step back and create unity, teamwork, and harmony.
Also, it's difficult for me to say sorry or admit when I'm wrong,
I dance away to the beat of my own drum… I sing my own song.

I do live for my family and friends though, I am extremely protective,
As the Lion I am a fierce protector of those I love, like my family and security.

My social and home life are important, I will always stand up for an underdog,
So remember this when you want to be on my bad side, for I am one of the most tough!

I am strong, charming, charismatic, and with great physical stamina,
People know not to mess with me because of my tough outward exterior.
But this isn't good for relationships, I tend to scare people away,
Friendships are short-lived and I ruin my reputation and fame.

A moment of unkindness, un-compassion, and insensitivity,
Can put out my ability to teach, inspire, and lead.
I don't like being a follower, therefore this is very hard for me to accept,
If you want to be my friend, you should remember I am dramatic as hell…

It's true, I really am a drama queen/king- I put on incredibly displays of theatrics,
My voice is louder than any other, and I shout and scream to win.
I want the spotlight, I want the crown; I am confident and mighty beyond belief,
Your job is to teach me how to be gracious, gentle, and more empathic in my speech.

Empathy is the opposite of aggression, coldness, and hostility,
It's a compassionate quality linked to teamwork, balance, and unity.
Empathy is the absence of greed and selfish motivations,
so you may be my teacher if you've mastered this sensation!

The paradox is, however, I will never admit I need help,
You must be an expert and master at emotional strength.
I am psychological, which signifies I "think" over "feel," moreover dismiss my insecurities,
I focus on my mind, wit, and charm more than any sentimentalities.

I am hard, not soft… strong, not weak, and brave, not cowardly,
The irony is sometimes my theatrics and temper make me act immaturely.
I can be child-like in my mannerisms, essentially like a baby,
So don't think this lion cub is only cute and cuddly!

My roar is deafening, I think softness is a weakness-

I also need to be admired on each and every level…
My pride and ego often get in the way of lasting relationships,
To find harmony with me, you will have to embrace multiple perspectives.

Please, guide me, show me how to be more modest,
I need help in calming down my inner zest.
I am overly passionate, way too dominant, and forceful in my ways,
I need people with grace and patience to help me evolve and change.

VIRGO: The Maiden

Key qualities: Orderly, practical, domestic, hard-working, responsible, down-to-earth, modest, organizational, reliable, patient, kind, trustworthy, disciplined, devoted, generous, intuitive, intelligent, logical, analytical, a problem-solver, perceptive, observant, and humble.

Weaknesses/Shadow traits to watch out for: Critical, cynical, a perfectionist, obsessive, excessive worry, stressed, judgmental, a 'know-it-all!'- prone to social anxiety and nervous tension, over-thinks, over-analyzes, and emotionally distant.

COMPATIBLE Star Signs: Taurus, Cancer, Virgo, Scorpio, Capricorn, and Pisces

INCOMPATIBLE, where there will be least harmony: Aries, Sagittarius, and Aquarius

I am Virgo, the Maiden- a symbol of purity, order, and sacredness,

2

I am the sign associated with structure and cleanliness!
I love to keep things clean, I am very practical,
I am responsible, full of duty, dependable, and methodological.

I love to pay attention to the finer details in life,
I am highly intelligent and observant, yet believe I'm always right!
Through my advanced wit, intellect, and logic,
I can be infuriating while believing I'm just honest.

I annoy people while thinking I know the best,
I like to constantly put my intelligence to the test…
Despite not being an official bully of the zodiac,
I put others down through superior intellect.

But I'm not actually superior, I'm just an annoying know-it-all,
I am cynical, highly critical, and smile at every fall.
I like seeing others struggle mentally and psychologically,
So I guess this does make me a bit of a bully!

However, I am kind, empathic, compassionate, and supremely modest,
Humility and sensitivity allow me to shine subtly, not conquer.
I don't need to bulldoze over others or shout to get my way,
I am sensitive and serene with a calm and cool brain.

At my best, I am cool, calm, and collected, which makes me bright,
I really am very down-to-earth despite believing myself to be right.
Hopefully you can teach me how to be less smug,
as my perfectionist nature prevents a magic touch.

But, I am also too kind and generous in this often cruel world,
I am one of the signs people walk over, I am treated like dirt…
I'm overlooked, underappreciated, and not valued as much as I should be,
I have a gentle heart and believe in helping a friend in need.

As the Maiden, a symbol for purity, I am devoted to my friends,
I dislike conflict and am a real helper, it's only my mind that drives people
round the bend!

I will never physically cause harm, I am not aggressive or hostile,
So remember this when I try to give you a smile.

The truth is, I am one of the most shy and reserved star signs,
I am humble, down-to-earth, and over-use my mind.
This means I overthink, I live in constant worry,
If I ever cause harm it's not consciously being a bully.

I have a lot of insecurities, I live in pessimism and low self-esteem,
I prefer to work towards harmony and be part of a team.
And this makes me overlooked, undervalued, and underappreciated,
This is when I turn cold- my thoughts become calculated.

I will dream and scheme up masterplots
to undermine your intelligence, which can put out your light and love.
I want to be seen as psychologically and intellectually superior, as this is my
saving grace,
It's the only thing that puts a smile back on my face.

At least, this is true when in my shadow, my lower mind-
My life lesson is to rise up to the divine.
Not everything is about perfection, structure, or order,
my highly practical nature can make friendships break down, it's a disaster...

I have a difficult time making friends because I alternate between shy and
rude,
Maybe you can help me be less reserved, and shine like you?
Or perhaps you can assist me in developing greater depth and vulnerability,
then no-one will have to be labeled as a victim or a bully.

LIBRA: The Scales

Key qualities: Charismatic, sociable, colorful, bubbly, charming, logical, analytical, intuitive, imaginative, innovative, friendly, sociable, romantic, kind, generous, comprising, cooperative, diplomatic, harmony-seeking, peace-loving, truth-bringing, just, fair, balanced, generous, empathic, tolerant, intellectual, and understanding.

Weaknesses/Shadow traits to watch out for: People-pleasing, indecisive, codependent, overly compromising, self-pity, escapes conflict, avoids confrontation, holds a grudge!- and super-sensitive.

COMPATIBLE Star Signs: Aries, Gemini, Leo, Libra, Sagittarius, and Aquarius

INCOMPATIBLE, where there will be least harmony: Cancer, Taurus, and Capricorn

Interesting fact! ~ Each star sign has an "opposite sign" they are supposed to find the most balance with. In Libra's case, their opposite sign is Aries, the most dominant, willful, and arguably bullyish sign of the Zodiac. So, Libra can find balance in Aries' qualities and strengths, when they want to be more decisive, assertive, and self-leading.

The other sign combinations are: Aries and Libra, Taurus and Scorprio, and Gemini and Sagittarius, Cancer and Capricorn, Leo and Aquarius, and Virgo and Pisces.

I am Libra, the sign of balance, fairness, and harmony,
I represent justice, cooperation, and diplomacy.
I am the person who will always try to keep the peace!
I despise conflict, it's the last thing I need.

In terms of exploring the bullies linked to astrology,
you should know that I stand against war, aggression, and hostility.
So, this means I will never, ever be the instigator,
I am empathic, kind, and a wonderful friend and protector.

I try to see all sides of a story, I don't turn against anyone,
I really hate gangs and cliques, I'm always the middle one…
These means I mediate and uses key skills of negotiation,
to make everyone feel seen, I don't succumb to the temptation…

… Of picking a winner or loser, or only seeing one person as right-
I believe there is unity to be found in every moment of fright.
As the sign of balance, justice, and harmony,
later in life I usually make an excellent judge, counselor, or truth speaker for unity!

I use my advanced communication and psychological gifts
To speak, lead, and teach, contributing to justice.
In school and youth, I always take the moral high ground,
which can make me sound superior, but, in truth, I just hate being loud.

I am colorful- I have a charismatic and outgoing personality,
However you'll never see me speak over anyone or outshine simply to lead.
Unless I am in a truly chaotic headspace, I will always try to find balance,
To show you and everyone the true meaning of kindness.

I am empathic, compassionate, and sensitive, yet deeply intellectual,
So try not to bully me when I'm showing you the meaning of friendship.
You see, I am one of the signs to be overpowered, despite my good intentions;
my real feelings and motives can be lost in translation.

I tend to people-please, falling into codependent traps,
This makes me vulnerable to less sensitive types…
As I am sensitive, humble, gentle, and nurturing,
may have many intellectual and logical gifts, but I am a softie with evolved compassion.

And I possess emotional intelligence, which means I live by inner harmony,
I've found balance between various states of duality.
Logic Vs intuition, wit Vs instinct, and thinking Vs feeling,
I am the star sign sent to show that multiple people can exist in…

… this game of life- there are so many cultures and personalities,
we don't have to outshine others and push others down if they can't lead.
Some people are leaders while others are followers,
Some people stand in the spotlight while others feel overpowered…
Some people are loud, boastful, courageous, and incredibly willful,
Yet others are shy and reserved, they don't know how to make their voice known.

Yet I am the one who sits comfortable in the middle, although I do receive backlash.
You may want me to pick a side, but, I'm sorry to say- I'm never in a rush!
I don't like making choices, I prefer to be a bit indecisive,
I am both extroverted and introverted, and expressive and passive.

So, please try not to turn against me if I can't choose a side,
I will always be a peace-keeper, even if it makes me cry.
I despise tension, fights, and conflict at all costs,
I am Libra, the Scales, a symbol for a white dove.

The white dove represents purity, faith, and intuition-
This is what I use when making hard decisions.
Life isn't always fair, some people will be left out,
My main goal is to make sure no-one gets extremely down.

It's naturally to have hard times, challenges are normal,

but life should never become an outright war!
Remember to ask for my advice when there are different opinions and needs,
for I am the only sign who stays neutral, I can't exist without harmony.

SCORPIO: The Scorpion

Key qualities: Independent, ambitious, hard-working, devoted, intelligent, observant, perceptive, wise, intuitive, artistic, imaginative, creative, loyal, generous, kind, romantic, sensitive, affectionate, nurturing, passionate, mysterious, spiritually aware, protective, courageous, compassionate, high-flying and achieving, disciplined, emotional mature, powerful, resourceful, and deep.

Weaknesses/Shadow traits to watch out for: Stubborn, possessive, vindictive, spiteful, a lack of remorse, moody, hyper-emotional, distrusting, jealous, and manipulative.

COMPATIBLE Star Signs: Taurus, Cancer, Virgo, Scorpio, Capricorn, and Pisces

INCOMPATIBLE, where there will be least harmony: Aries, Gemini, and Aquarius

I am Scorpio, the willful yet sensitive Scorpion,
I am a contradiction in character because I have two planetary rulers!
This means that, unlike other signs, I am both fire and water,
Mars is my ancient ruler while Pluto is more modern.

Mars' influence makes me fiery, passionate, and courageous,
I am competitive and forceful- I live to be the best.
I can be aggressive and domineering, moreover overly energetic,
which makes me blunt instead of slowing down or being reflective.

Mars is Aries' current planetary ruler, the sign of war,
Conflict, action, and a primitive force.
This makes me crave security and survival that can put out the light,
I can be arrogant and boastful while believing I'm always right.

But, Pluto is my modern day ruler, and this gives me sensitivity;
Water is empathic, gentle, and emotional, you see.
Pluto helps me to see with higher eyes,
It's not all about competition, but compassion and the sublime.

Tranquility, a need for peace, and loyalty are part of my personality,
So I do offer a harmonious touch- I possess humility and diplomacy.
In saying this, even water can be explosive…
I am determined to succeed and incredibly ambitious.

So, I want to shine and be seen as talented and gifted,
I might be sensitive and gracious, yet I am also highly imaginative.
When at the top of my game, I need to gather close friends,
Luckily, I am not one of the most bullyish, if I am it's just a trend.

In the end, I will always stand up for underdog and try to remain kind,
It's not in my nature to outshine
everyone, I need friendship, connection, and community;
If you ever see me being a bully, check the other people around me.

I can be negatively influenced, you see, and this is due to wanting love.

In my desires for friendship and company, I may put out my own magic
touch.
As, at my best I am a soulful warrior, a very modest and honest friend,
I am not so ambitious or willful that I drive others round the bend.

But, watch out! This Scorpion has its sting, so I will always protect-
I will defend myself and my loved ones, so be warned if you start conflict.
I don't like tyrannical characters who want to be the only best,
If you disrupt the balance and harmony it will put my strength to the test...

My temper can be explosive, and I am known for being vindictive,
For turning spiteful and incredibly manipulative,
If I sense foul play, dirty tricks, or mean actions,
I will show you what it's like to be on the other end of the spectrum.

I am usually shy and reserved, preferring to blend into the crowd,
I am expressive and passionate, but not very loud.
I may appear odd, strange, or simply a misfit,
which makes others overlook me or start negative gossip.

I have a few close friends, but I am not one to boast-
I don't like superficial connections, I prefer to be on my own.
So, this can leave me open to negativity and harsh words,
People tend to look down on me for being the oddball, the lone wolf...

I do become a bully when it's to teach others a lesson,
as I am the one who fights back once there is havoc and chaos!
If you don't want to change or grow up, watch out! I may be your karma,
I can hold a grudge for an eternity... My need for revenge outlives anything
saint-like or harmonious.

SAGITTARIUS: The Centaur

Key qualities: Charming, charismatic, innovative, intuitive, intelligent, expressive, passionate, wise, discerning, creative, idealistic, visionary, powerful, ambitious, courageous, fearless, excitable, enthusiastic, travel-loving, adventurous, spontaneous, honest, fun-loving, playful, a free spirit, energetic, optimistic, and generous.

Weaknesses/Shadow traits to watch out for: Egotistical, bullyish, fanatic, self-righteous, self-entitled, aggressive, domineering, overpowering, lacks sensitivity and empathy, blunt, frivolous, impatient, reckless, and impulsive.

COMPATIBLE Star Signs: Aries, Gemini, Leo, Libra, Sagittarius, and Aquarius

INCOMPATIBLE, where there will be least harmony: Cancer, Virgo, and Pisces

Fun Fact: Some signs have two planetary rulers, an "ancient" one and a "modern" one. If your star sign has an ancient ruler, you can read up on the star sign linked to your ancient ruler! For example, Pisces is currently ruled by *Neptune*, but has *Jupiter* as an ancient ruler. This means *Pisces* can read up on *Sagittarius* to discover deeper aspects to their personality. This adds an extra dimension to your learning activities…

The same is true for Scorpio (current ruler Pluto; ancient ruler Mars) and Aquarius (current ruler Uranus; ancient ruler Saturn).

3

I am Sagittarius, the fiery and expressive Archer,
I am bold and energetic with the symbol of the Centaur.
I have two symbols, and both represent different things;
One represents my ability to shoot for the stars... the other is my sins!

I am full of life force, I possess immense creative vision,
Yet I also have too much energy, which makes me act from instinct.
I can be impulsive and impatient, moreover quick to anger,
I am known for being blunt, o.t.t., and full of slander.

I like to have fun and play, but this makes me reckless-
immature, ungrounded, and totally careless...
I am frivolous, fun-loving, and very extroverted,
I lack all sense of responsibility and can be a mean-spirited nasty jerk.

Oh yes, I am one of the aggressive ones, and this is because I am born of fire
I don't know how to cool it down and possess a wild inner spirit.
I like to lead, I don't like to follow, and I am very dominant;
which means I am unkind when it comes to other people's song.

I always need to shout, speak, and sing,
I don't let others do their own thing.
I am smug and arrogant, I have a massive ego,
This ultimately signifies I put on a show.

As I am highly passionate and expressive,
I need to be seen as a boss, yet I'm not selfless.
So, I seek the spotlight, also believing I'm always right.
Did I say I have a big ego? This makes me a bully,
I am one of the signs to make others feel small and weak- I'm so pushy!

I am fearless, brave, and honest, however,
I have many strengths... When at my best, I am an amazing friend;
I am creative, intelligent, open-minded, and concerned with higher things-
Like philosophy, reaching for the stars, and culture,
I like learning, expanding my horizons, and traveling wide and far...

But, I do tend to treat others as my doormat,
I am selfish, big-headed, and not that soft.
I lack gentleness and humility, least to mention grace-
Others feeling suppressed puts a smile on my face.

I like having lots of minions, you see, fairness is not my true nature,
and I don't like harmony or cooperation- I prefer to be the leader;
to teach, inspire, and gain lots of followers,
I need you to tame down my wild side, so I can gain trust.

Because I'm not too trustworthy,
Sometimes I am your friend and other times I'm your foe...
The truth is, I love to steal the show!

Being so impatient and impulsive makes me act brashly,
I lack depth, nurturing, and sensitivity.
In fact, I am so insensitive that I am usually the head of a gang,
I don't mind making others feel worthless or rejecting them.

Overly self-confident, annoying, loud, and rude,
my self-assertiveness is taken to new levels, I am quite crude.
This means I don't care what I say or how or say it, or how I act;
It makes me act like a child, a selfish little brat...

When at my best I am a loyal and honest friend- I'm the life and soul of the party,
I'm colorful, bold, imaginative, full of new ideas, and inspiring!
But, you will need to be both honest and blunt to handle my hostility,
as my lesson in life is to embody more depth, vulnerability, and humility.

CAPRICORN: The Earth Goat

Key qualities: Disciplined, hard-working, determined, tenacious, practical, generous, kind, selfless, sophisticated, grounded, down-to-earth, modest, humble, gracious, elegant, wise, discerning, logical, intuitive, instinctive, reliable, trustworthy, responsible, resourceful, observant, perceptive, confident, self-motivated, charming, high flying and achieving, ambitious, success-driven, patient, helpful, and self-controlled.

Weaknesses/Shadow traits to watch out for: Overly concerned with status, image, money, power, and prestige… stubborn, obsessive, inability to relax, stressed, workaholic!- unforgiving, pessimistic, and a 'know-it-all.'

I am Capricorn the earth Goat,
When at my worst I gloat!
I am smug, pretentious, and completely delusional
As for other people's intelligence, I think I am the only one skilled in…

… Logic, intellect, higher reasoning, wit, and problem-solving,
I believe I am intellectually superior, and it turns me cold and condescending.
You see, I am the sign associated with ambition,
I am wise, strong-willed, and incredibly determined.

I'm tenacious and preserving, I work hard to achieve my goals,
This makes me neglect friendships in the pursuit of gold.
I crave money, security, fame, and prestige,
I'm happy to follow, but I prefer to lead.

I have a business mind, even from a young age,
which makes my relationships suffer in the name of fortune and fame.
So, at school and home I tend to dominate and suppress,
I enjoy being seen as intellectual, the best.

I lack emotional vulnerability- I am unable to show my feelings,
I'd rather suppress them and focus on my achievements.
But, this isn't healthy, as it makes me suppress others,
To put out their light, their joy, and their courage!

Sometimes it's conscious and other times it's not,
In truth, I don't have a very tranquil touch.
I am always on the go, always busy looking to accomplish and conquer.
I am incapable of rest or fun, so being playful is not my nature.

And this makes the teacher's pet, the goodie two shoes, and the know it all!

I don't care who else is sad as long as I don't fall...
I am incredibly humble, however, modesty is one of my strengths,
I'm down-to-earth, generous, kind, and full of zest.

I don't mind others being great and mighty, as long as it doesn't get in the way of my path-
If they do, well, let's just say good luck with this horned Goat.
My symbol is the Goat who can, quite literally, walk up steep mountains;
I have horns for defense, which signifies my strong nature.

I become a bully when I feel others are stealing the spotlight,
I am harmonious and peace-loving yet won't let others shine.
My future career and dream life comes first, every single time,
I don't care how many people I trod over to get to the finish line.

I am not aggressive in a fiery or explosive way,
But I can be impatient and act from overbearing instincts, it's my way or the highway!
So, take note if you want to be friend, I may look down on you-
I am sorry to say but I will always be cold and rude.

Even when I clearly love you and want to make the friendship work,
Nothing will ever, ever, come in the way of place in the world.
As I am the ambitious mountain Goat who chooses education and career over intimacy,
I need company and companionship, but lack sensitivity.

I am cold, heartless, callous, and extremely calculated in my ways,
I'll sometimes show off my personal power in dramatic displays...
Of self-autonomy, confidence, and a down-to-earth type of power,
try not to get in my way of success and overuse of power.

But, if you are my friend, I will need a gentle touch; be brave!
Show me there's more to life than status, money, and fame.
And, please, don't ever criticize me, as it may put you in the firing line,
The one thing I despise is someone trying to change or control my mind.

If you must offer me advice to help me, do it with the utmost sensitivity,
Act with grace, gentleness, and humility.
Speak as if you know nothing, and are just suggesting a new idea,
because I am so headstrong and stubborn I will make you live in fear…

I am the sign of self-autonomy, you see- I hate being told what to do.
I am happy to give advice but can't receive it, it's a real issue!
create my own path and live by my own terms, so never judge or put me down
or you might just find yourself in big trouble, I don't like people messing with my Crown.

4

AQUARIUS: The Water-Bearer

Key qualities: Idealistic, visionary, intuitive, original, inventive, innovative, intellectual, intelligent, bright, witty, humorous, adventurous, spontaneous, communicative, passionate, expressive, logical, analytical, imaginative, perceptive, wise, observant, charming, charismatic, friendly, independent, cultured, unique, open-minded, creative, and sociable.

Weaknesses/Shadow traits to watch out for: Self-centered, selfish, egotistical, aggressive, impulsive, reckless, a rebel, ungrounded, impractical, emotionally aloof and distant, incapable of depth or real feelings, cold, and ruthless.

COMPATIBLE Star Signs: Aries, Gemini, Leo, Libra, Sagittarius, and Aquarius

INCOMPATIBLE, where there will be least harmony: Cancer, Virgo, and Scorpio

I am Aquaius, the Water-Bearer, I have many bullyish traits,
This is because I am a "yang" sign, I am full of passion and zest.
Energy spiraled out-of-control creates an aggressive personality,
I can be impulsive, impatient, quick to anger, or full of hostility!

I am an inventive and original air sign, which makes me very curious,
I like to explore new ideas, be philosophical, and commit to a course
of action, I love exploring new cultures and languages-
I am deeply bright and intelligent, but this gives me some doubts and fears…

And I don't like people knowing my fears, so this brings out my inner bully-
I pretend I have it all together, but, deep down, I'm full of insecurity.
I want to change the world, I am a visionary and a dreamer!
Yet I am deeply impatient, so I have a hard time accepting that the grass is greener…

On my side, I always want to live in the future,
to plot and dream up the next scheme that will make the world less meaner.
I live for idealism, vision, and a utopian view of how our earth can be,
I desperately want everyone to be happy and free.

But I want it now, now… now!- this makes me very irrational,

I can become rude and even tyrannical.
So, I am a contradiction in terms, wanting a more harmonious world
while acting from impulse and anger, preventing true evolution to occur.

I am ahead of my years, very pragmatic, and full of original concepts,
Yet at school and home I am reserved, actually, I'm socially awkward!
I am the oddball and black sheep, the loner-
I love my solitude and have a hard time accepting my worth.

I then lash out on others from feeling misunderstood,
I think the world is against me, when really I am just a jerk!
Because I'm cold and aggressive, rude and withdrawn too,
I don't like sharing my feelings or letting anyone in on my mood.

I am shy, sensitive, introspective, solitude-loving, and a bit depressed,
I give into negative thinking while pretending to be the best.
I give off a vibe of intellectual superiority, you see,
which secretly makes others dislike or hate me.

As, I think I am the only one with bright or inventive ideas,
At my best I am imaginative and witty with the intelligence of a seer.
Yet, in youth I have many follies to work through, just like everyone else;
My desires for world peace and unity prevent me from being my best.

When I feel neglected, pushed aside, or simply ignored
I will break things, act out, and smash doors…
Oh yes, I have a real problem with calming down my anger,
I want everyone to see my frustrations through physical displays of power.

So, I become a bully, scaring others with my strength,
I can turn others against me and then pretend
It's their fault, I adopt the belief that 'life isn't fair;'
I play victim and then all hell breaks loose, because I am the one causing
havoc…
Creating chaos, negativity, hatred, and destruction…

My lesson, therefore, is to learn to work on my feelings,

To develop and strengthen empathy coupled with emotional wisdom.
I need to be more vulnerable with my friends and loved ones,
Only then will I stop being reckless and become one of the Chosen Ones.

PISCES: The Fish

Key qualities: Impressionable, sweet, sensitive, nurturing, caring, compassionate, unconditionally loving, wise, honest, multitalented, spiritually perceptive, intuitive, imaginative, a creative genius, mystical, adaptable, a dreamer, visionary, prophetic, psychic, empathic, emotionally vulnerable and open, deep, soulful, majestic, kind, understanding, patient, loving, non-judgmental, smart, merciful, expressive, selfless, and inspirational.

Weaknesses/Shadow traits to watch out for: Naive, gullible, too innocent, overly trusting, ungrounded, impractical, moody, escapes and avoids conflicts, hyper-emotional, super-sensitive, and self-sacrificing.

COMPATIBLE Star Signs: Taurus, Cancer, Virgo, Scorpio, Capricorn, and Pisces

INCOMPATIBLE, where there will be least harmony: Gemini, Leo, and Sagittarius

I am Pisces, the two Fish swimming in opposite directions,
This represents my fluid and passive nature- I can't make decisions!
I try to escape harsh experiences and situations,
and isolate myself so people don't see my frustrations.

I am incredibly sensitive, you see, one of the most shy,
I am kind, humble, compassionate, and see from a higher eye.
This means I have a spiritual essence, I am connected to invisible realms,
am in tune with the subconscious and dreams… I am deeply concerned with my soul.

But this makes me ungrounded, as well as distanced from reality-
I replace material needs and necessities with faraway spirituality.
I am philosophical, open-minded, loving, and deeply wise,
Yet I lack the physical strength and stamina to stand my ground, or be less kind!

I am too kind- too trusting and giving,
My sweet and nurturing personality makes me bait to others' drilling...
I often get ridiculed, ganged up on, slandered, and left out;
I am the lone wolf and oddball, the black sheep without a gang.

I tend to be a loner, finding comfort in my own mind,
In my emotions, my imagination, the sublime, and the divine.
I exist in another world- I day dream often,
and I am very intelligent and intuitive, which makes me a pawn in other's destruction.

People often pick me out because they know I am weak,
Being humble, selfless, and gentle is seen as a weakness to others, you see.
They know I can be used, they are aware I can be victimized,
I lack the communication skills and willpower to bring bullying into the light.

So, I suffer in silence, getting lost in the realm of fantasy,
of imagination, artistic gifts, introspection, dreams, and creativity.
This doesn't help my self-esteem, however, as everybody needs friends!

5

I really hope everyone stops picking on me… I have a lot of unique gifts to share.

In fact, I am multi-talented, and I guess this is why I am picked on,
while others are shouting or being fake for attention I am truly honest.
I am not egotistical or boastful in my abilities to be brilliant or connect to ancient knowledge.
Also, as a shy and sensitive water sign I am extremely emotional…

Hypersensitive, lost in fantasy, sentimental, and highly irrational.
This makes me an easy target, quite simply. I am usually treated as a doormat.
Down-trodden and depressed, sad and upset, I lack assertiveness and strong will,
I tend to pick up on other people being sad, angry, or ill.

It's a sixth sense, a psychic gift, and inner knowing and intuition-
I am the sign associated with higher wisdom and vision!
So, people look down on me, as I am something they're not used to,
I'm not one of the loudest, nor will I curse or be rude.

I am gracious, angelic, saintlike, and overly selfless,
Louder personalities sense I may secretly be the best.
I am the zodiac's victim, the one who will always be left out,
I'm pushed into isolation and am made to believe the world isn't fair.

But, you should know, no-one in life is a victim- we create our fate,
I do have the strength, moreover the power to rise up and create
the life I long for, making use of my creative talents;
Just please, give me a chance, be kind and patient- I'm not a tyrant!

I will never shout or bulldoze over others to get my way,
I will stand back and give others a chance to shine, I am humble without complaint…
I will never join in on someone else being bullied either, unless I've truly had enough,

I am compassion and love personified with the grace of a dove.

In saying all this, watch out: I am connected to the infinite sea and unknown,
Like the fish who swim freely, the ocean is truly my home.
This means I'm connected to a subtle and ancient power,
I will not let anyone physically harm me, so be careful if you try to.

Because I am one of the silently deadly ones who will one day rule the world,
I may be shy and overlooked in youth, yet, in the future, I am a star!
Pisces is the 12th and last sign, representing the evolution of the soul;
Be mindful bullies, your time is coming… No hate, but karma is real.

Afterword

Congratulations, young one!
You have completed your journey to discover your Star Sign.
Now you have much more wisdom than when you started,
You are now aware of the deeper parts of your personality, your psyche.
Nomatter what this world presents you, remember you are part of a greater plan;
You are a cosmic child of the universe, a divine young woman or man...
You come from the stars, you are destined for more than the mundane-
Astrology will help you gain abundance, money, and fame.
Or simply find strength in the stars up above,
while bringing you peace, the tranquility of a dove.
Hidden secrets and insights are now coming to light,
so you don't have to live in fear or flight.
You may not understand this now, but one day you will realize the following is true:
We all have a shine and a shadow, there's a light and dark part to you.

It's only when we make peace with our inner darkness that we can find our light;
This is where true magic and connection arises, and when we shine bright!
So, take this wisdom into your wonderful future, remembering we are *all* the student and the teacher.
No-one is more or less superior, we all have different gifts and strengths,
And try to work on your weaknesses so you're not the bully or only 'best.'
We all deserve to shine, we all have a right to life;
Astrology is a secret chord to the most valuable knowledge, and it all begins inside...

A Zodiac-Wisdom Book for Kids: HOW TO OVERCOME BULLYING, FIND FAIRNESS & HARMONY, AND TAKE BACK YOUR POWER!

Key Life Lessons for ALL Home, School, and Social/Peer Group Scenarios

Author/Poet: *GRACE GABRIELLA PUSKAS*
Artist/Illustrator: *HUSNA LOHIYA*

Printed in Great Britain
by Amazon